MY
LITTLE GIRL
Julia Finds Happiness in the U.S.

by

Rimma Mello

Narrative by Julia M. Mello

ISBN-13: 978-0996054935
ISBN-10: 0996054936

©Copyright 2014 W.O.M.B. PUBLICATIONS
Jersey City, New Jersey

Edited by Raymond Harris

Photos by Rimma Mello and Carol Ellison

Cover design created by Raymond Harris

W.O.M.B. PUBLICATIONS

All rights reserved

Thanks to Mr. and Mrs. Raymond and Desiree' Harris and my close friend Carol Ellison for encouraging me to write this book.

In memory of my daughter, Julia Musailova-Mello (1978-2012) who loved nature, art and everything that was beautiful in life. Born in Latvia, lived in Brooklyn, worked for HBO TV (New York).

Hi my name is Julia. This is a picture of me when I was little.

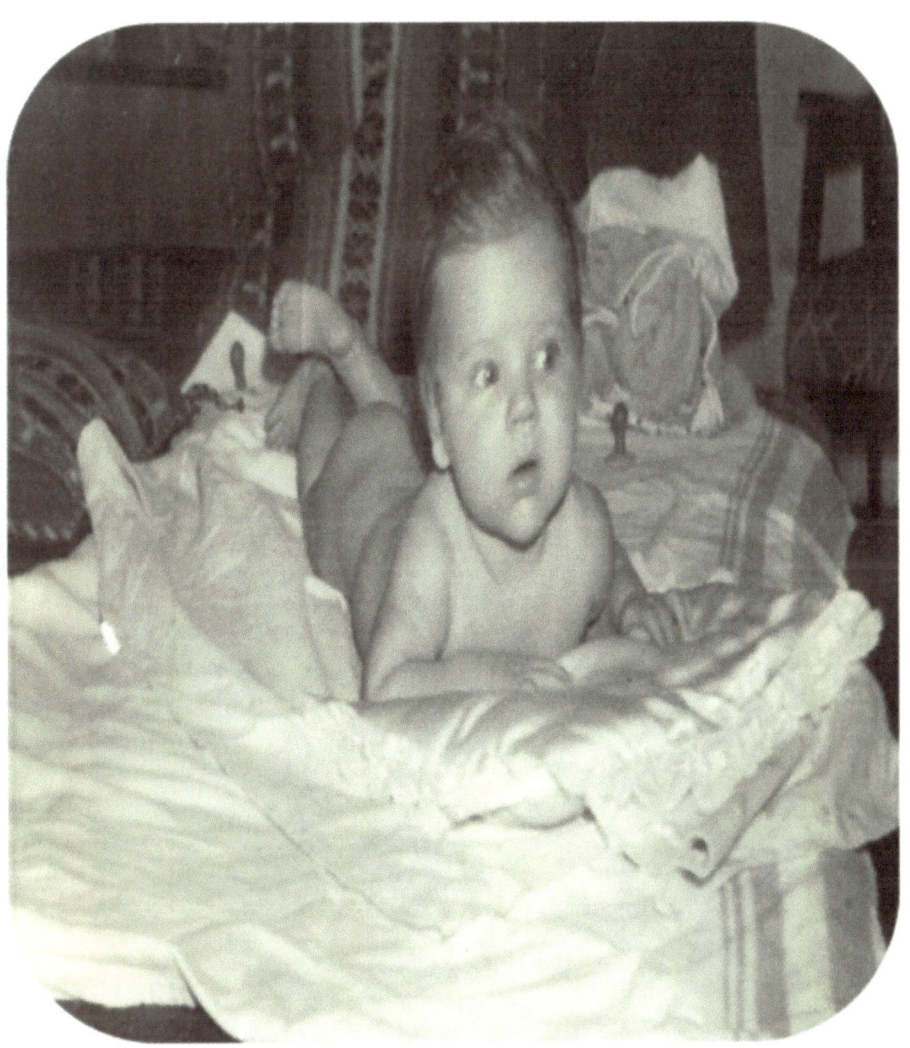

I was born in the country called Latvia.

In which country were you born?

This is my favorite street in Riga, Latvia.

My parents spoke only in Russian. For example:

- страна – country
- язык – language
- родители – parents
- говорить – speak
- Латвия – Latvia

What language do your parents speak?

My favorite toy was Vanjka-Vstanjka. This toy made pretty musical sounds!

Did you have a favorite toy when you were little?

I liked to sit on my favorite high chair.

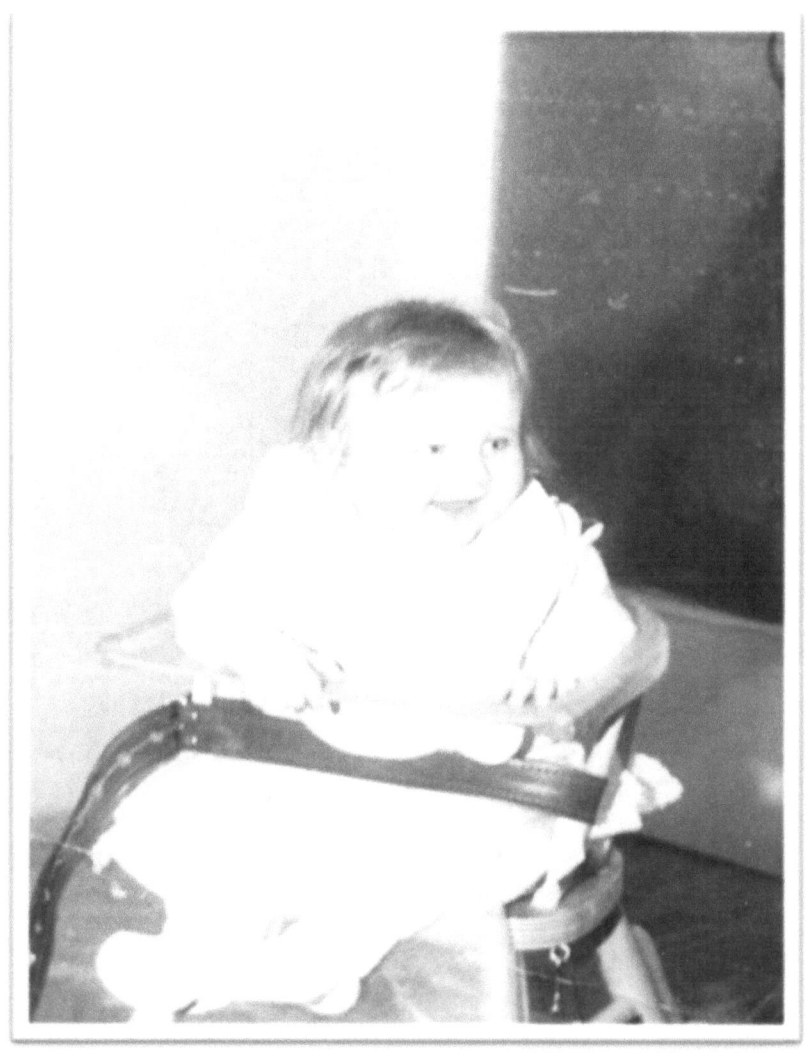

Sometimes I smiled....

My Little Girl

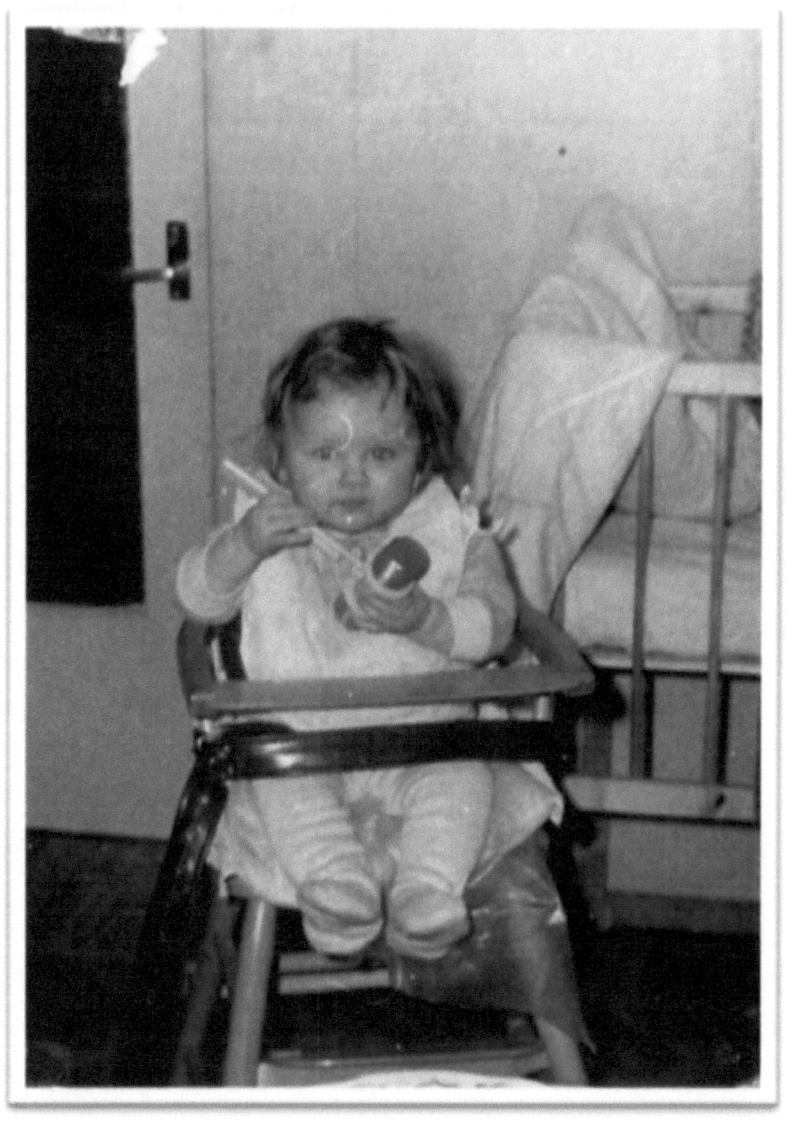

...and sometimes I was very serious.

Rimma Mello

I had two grandmothers, Nina

My Little Girl

and Valja.

They loved me very much. Neither of them ever moved from Latvia.

My grandfathers Rant and Aleksej lived in Latvia too.

My Little Girl

We liked to spend time together.

What do you like to do with your grandparents?

My cousin Galia was taller than me...

....and I was taller than my cousin Ira.

I liked to draw on the sand with my friend Danik.

Did you ever draw on the wet sand?

In my preschool I loved singing with my friends.

My favorite song was about Peace in the World and Sunny Days for All People!

I liked to dance by the Christmas tree as well.

Do you like to dance and sing songs at school?

Rimma Mello

When I was 13, I had to leave my friends....

...and family behind, in Latvia.

I missed them very much.

But soon I found American friends in my new school.

Many of them grew up in different countries: Ecuador, Egypt, Russia, and Ukraine.

Because of my closest friends Mohammad, Dolores, Rita, Max, and Andrei, my life in America became richer and happier.

Do you have friends at your school? How do they make you feel?

I go to Latvia to visit my family and cousins very often.

Galia and Ira are grown-ups now like me!

My best friend Christina (who lives in Latvia) comes to America to visit me very often as well. We do many wonderful things together!

What do you like to do with your best friends?

Christina now has a little girl, Lisa.....

.....who is growing up in Latvia.

My Little Girl

I often wondered to myself.......

.....will she also come to live in America?

What do YOU think?

About the Author

Rimma Mello was born in Riga, the capital city of Latvia near Russia, in 1954. She came to the U.S. to visit a friend in 1993 where she would meet her husband-to-be, and took up permanent residency in America. Ten months later her 13 year old daughter Julia, would join her in the states and they would begin their new life.

Unfortunately Julia's life would be cut short in 2012 at the tender age of 33. Her loss would inspire Rimma to write this book *"My Little Girl"* to allow her daughters friends as well as their children and others to know of the rich and happy life she experienced here in America as a young girl, all the way into her adulthood, before meeting her untimely death.

Rimma wants to share with the reader her daughter's experience by using Julia's own eyes and voice as the narrative from beginning to end, to let others know how coming to a new place can be challenging in the beginning, but with patience and perseverance, better and brighter days do unfold, as Julia found in America a very rich and happy life full of many friendships and successful endeavors.

Rimma still resides in the US today as a preschool teacher fulltime, and as a new author of children's' books, with the recent 2014 release of her published book *"We Have a Problem, Let's Solve It"*. She is a proud mother who continually strives to keep the memory of her daughter alive.

Check out More Titles from our W.O.M.B. PUBLICATIONS' Authors!

We Have a Problem: Let's Solve it!
by Rimma Mello

- and -

What We do in Preschool

Zakiyah's "My Big Happy Family"
by Desiree' Monique

- also -

How to Earn and Save Money
by Khalis J. Harris

- and -

The Takeoff Show Comic Book
by Mikal Harris

For Orders visit our website at:

www.wombpublications.com

For info contact:

Raymond Harris - Editor in Chief

W.O.M.B. Publications

Giving Birth to the Best Books on Earth!

www.ingramcontent.com/pod-product-compliance
Lightning Source LLC
Chambersburg PA
CBHW041809040426
42449CB00001B/28